RUGBY

TENNESSEE'S VICTORIAN VILLAGE

DOUG& DAWN BRACHEY

HISTORIC RUGBY
P.O. Box 8 ◆ Rugby, TN 37733
(615) 628-2441

Updates: Historic Rugby tours, food service, lodging and museum stores are now open daily year round. Holidays closed are Thanksgiving, Christmas Eve, Christmas Day and New Year's Day. The annual Pilgrimage is now held on the first full weekend in October. Christmas At Rugby is now open to the general public.

Printing & Binding: Jostens, Clarksville, Tennessee

Foreword

Finally, after countless requests, here is the republication of the first (and to date, only) color photograph book on Tennessee's Rugby. Read it...study the pictures...and you will see why Rugby remains one of America's most fascinating historic sites.

That Rugby and its heritage can captivate, even inspire, is evident in its century-long human history. First there was Thomas Hughes, the famous English author and social reformer upon whose dreams and ideals the colony was founded. Then came the settlers—second sons, families, widows and spinsters, teachers, doctors, craftsmen, tradesmen—all bound together by the desire to "begin life anew."

As the decades passed, the early keepers of Rugby's heritage emerged —Will and Sarah Walton, Nelly Lender Brooks, Helen Turner, Patricia and Hugo Wichmann, Thula Justice, Helen Lourie, James Keen, Oscar, Allen Palmer and Irving Martin—some of them sons and daughters of original colonists.

Then in the mid-1960's, a 16-year-old-boy from nearby Deer Lodge resolved to begin what others had dreamed of—the permanent restoration and preservation of the entire village and its history. With the help of area residents and people across Tennessee, Brian Stagg formed the Rugby Restoration Association in 1966. Under a decade of his leadership, Christ Church Episcopal, the Thomas Hughes Library, Kingstone Lisle and the Board of Aid land office were restored. Daily historic building tours were started in 1968. In 1972 the entire village was named to the National Register of Historic Places. Carefully thought out plans were formulated to restore and historically reconstruct more of the village. When Brian's life ended in 1976, Tennessee and the nation were beginning to realize Rugby's cultural importance and its uniqueness as a truly unspoiled historic community.

Brian had shared his dreams for Rugby's future with many people, and some stepped in to continue the work of renamed Historic Rugby. In the past two decades, the museum and preservation organization has restored the Schoolhouse and installed "story of Rugby" exhibitry there, and historically reconstructed the original Rugby Commissary, Percy Cottage and the Board of Aid land office (after it was destroyed by fire in 1977). The colony's first boarding facility, Newbury House, has been restored for visitor lodging, as has Pioneer Cottage, where Thomas Hughes stayed on his first visit to his new colony. The Rugby Printing Works has been restored and furnished with 19th century printing equipment. A new, historically compatible Harrow Road Cafe has been built for area residents and visitors. A carefully formulated, award-winning *Master Plan for the Preservation, Protection, Management and Development of the Rugby Colony Historic District* has been produced to help guide Rugby's next century.

The plan's land use recommendations and design guidelines have guided both private owners and Historic Rugby in restoration and new construction work throughout the historic district. The most exciting example is Beacon Hill at Historic Rugby, a homesite development where new "colonists" can again buy lots and build architecturally compatible homes in Rugby. The 40-acre tract was originally lotted off and designated for residential building on the official town map in the 1880's , with plans for walking trails and a village bandstand that are realities today.

As the colonists found more than a century ago, the Rugby townsite is in a region of unsurpassed natural beauty, surrounded on three sides by river gorges and sandstone bluffs. Immediately adjacent is the 105,000-acre Big South Fork National River & Recreation Area, with more than 300 miles of hiking, biking and equestrian trails. Nearby are Frozen Head and Pickett State Parks, Colditz Cove State Natural Area and the Obed Wild and Scenic River.

What of Rugby's future plans and dreams? The continuing care and preservation of the public historic buildings and their settings is of paramount importance. So is the continued restoration and care of private historic homes by their owners. Several more buildings will be historically reconstructed in the coming years. Perrigo Boarding House, torn down decades ago, will be used for seminars, retreats and visitor lodging. And, of course, the ultimate reconstruction goal is the Tabard Inn, whose foundation stones are still visible above the Clear Fork River.

Some of Historic Rugby's exciting education goals include construction of an auditorium and amphitheatre where films, skits and plays will help tell Rugby's story. Funds are being raised to buy and restore Uffington House, where Thomas Hughes aged mother and young niece lived from 1881-1887, for daily living history interpretation. A landscape master plan will gradually be implemented which preserves original plants and trees and further improves pathways and parking throughout the village.

Living throughout America and other countries are hundreds of descendants of Rugby's early colonists. Many of them are in touch with Historic Rugby and have furnished historic pictures, letters and family records that are vitally important to the continuing effort to preserve Rugby's human story. But many more are "out there," perhaps in possession of important historic material and possibly unaware of Rugby's renaissance. Perhaps the republication of this book will help establish contact with some of them.

Non-profit Historic Rugby and the Rugby community continue to strive to achieve something rare in America today—preservation of an entire historic village and its setting and permanent protection from incompatible development. Every day, visitors and residents help the effort by becoming members, volunteering, shopping at the museum stores, lodging in historic buildings, eating at the Harrow Road Cafe, taking the guided tour, attending events and workshops and donating to special fundraising efforts.

We invite you to take part in the continuing story of Rugby as our second century unfolds.

Barbara Stagg, Executive Director
April, 1995

4

Thomas Hughes, founder of Rugby.

In 1880, as two continents watched, famous English author and social reformer Thomas Hughes launched his new American colony — Rugby, Tennessee. For one brief moment, Thomas Hughes' Rugby shone brightly. It bustled and bulged with residents and visitors alike. From laughing and splashing at the Gentlemen's Swimming Hole to quiet worship at Christ Church, Rugby's citizens enjoyed a rich cultural and social life.

Thomas Hughes, the second son of John and Margaret Hughes, attended Rugby School in England from 1833 to 1841. The charismatic headmaster of Rugby School, Thomas Arnold, had a great influence on Hughes. Arnold's public school reform was brought before the public and Hughes came to international prominence through the 1857 publication of his autobiographical classic, *Tom Brown's School Days.*

5

Rugby School in England.

Hughes was a versatile individual, deeply concerned about his fellow man. Among his many accomplishments were his admission to the bar in 1848, the founding of London Working Men's College in 1854, his election as Member of Parliament, and appointment as Queen's Counsel to Victoria in 1869. Throughout his life, Hughes was concerned with trade unions and the cooperative movement. An idealist, Hughes dreamed of utopia. His optimism was seen most clearly in the founding of Rugby, Tennessee.

Hughes envisioned an experimental village that would have "its own store and common church, both set in the quiet comfort of an old-fashioned village in England." The community would "house gentlemen and ladies, where all to some extent would work with their hands, and where even the humblest would be cultured enough to meet princes." The town would be free of the "evils of competitive trade" and "intoxicating liquors . . . will be strictly prohibited." Religious freedom would be guaranteed to all citizens.

Hughes dreamed of a way to help "second sons." In England it was customarily the elder sons who inherited the family title and estate. Second sons were to act as if they had an inheritance, while in reality they were left with a meager allowance and were discouraged from entering all but a few socially-acceptable professions such as law, medicine, ministry, or the military.

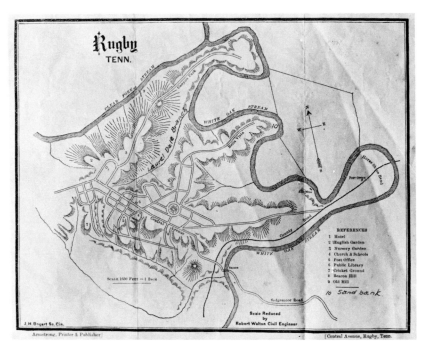

Town map of Rugby.

These fields were extremely crowded, and the second sons were mostly left without a means of livelihood. Hughes hoped that in Rugby second sons could be merchants, farmers, and laborers without shame. They could have self-esteem in doing a job well and in earning their own living.

After nearly a decade of dreaming and planning, what seemed to be the perfect spot for the colony was found. During bad economic times, a Boston company had to lay off many of its workers, and planned to resettle them on the Cumberland Plateau in Tennessee. However, before the workers could resettle, the economy improved, the workers returned to their jobs, and the Boston Board of Aid to Land Ownership began to look for a buyer for this Tennessee land.

In November 1878, Thomas Hughes, having heard of this Tennessee land through his friend, American poet James Russell Lowell, sent British barrister John Boyle to inspect the site. Boyle traveled to the site on the newly-built Cincinnati-Southern Railway, and filed a very favorable report:

> The climate . . . in November . . . is delightful during the day with a sunshine sometimes quite powerful for the time of year . . . I felt that I had reached a pure and more genial atmosphere and temperature . . . which at once attracted me favourably towards the climate.
>
> The soil also pleased me . . . It was . . . easily cultivated, appearing to yield readily . . . very fine corn, clover, potatoes, apples, cabbages, tobacco, and other produce. . . . It did not seem to be laborious cultivation which had been used, but the very slightest and least artificial.
>
> The noble timber was a constant theme of my wonder and admiration.

It would be difficult to find a country presenting so many favourable positions for establishing a large scheme of colonization, whether in town, manufacturing, farming, or residential sites, as soon as the railroad now being constructed to and over a considerable portion of the table land, has been completed.

[Of the] Six specimens of the coals ... five have proved to be of a quality which will yield a strong and good coke.

[There is an] ... abundance of grasses on which cattle and sheep feed contentedly ... and ... droves of hogs abound, fattening inexpensively on luxuriant fruits of the beech, oak, chestnut, and hickory.

Nature has liberally supplied this charming land, which only awaits the hand and intellect of man to awaken it to a prodigious fertility. I rejoice to think that ... given your sound scheme for peopling those lovely and now lonely woodlands... will be rewarded by seeing noble results in busy factories, thriving homesteads, and healthy centres, destined to arise and yield bread and happiness to a population.

October 5, 1880 — Rugby was "officially opened." In his address on that opening day, Thomas Hughes stated:

We are about to open a town here — in other words to create a new centre of human life ... in this strangely beautiful solitude.... Our settlement is open to all who like our principles and our ways, and care to come here to make homes for themselves .... There is this lovely corner of God's earth which has been intrusted to us ... treat it lovingly and reverently. We can add little, perhaps, to its natural beauty, but at least we can be careful to spoil it as little as possible .... Buildings ... must be simple and even rough in materials and construction. But there is no reason whatever why they should not, at the same time, be sightly and good in form and proportion .... In one word, our aim and hope are to plant on these highlands a community of gentlemen and ladies.

Opening day festivities included this poem which was symbolic of the new ties between old England and young America:

Long years and years, the wilderness, in regal beauty slept
As did the enchanted Princess, whom the bands of Faerie kept
In slumber for a century, until a princely knight
Should come to break that bondage with his glance of love and light ...
For why! The princely knight has come, so loyal and so true,
With love light from the Old World as a blessing to the New.

by Mrs. L. Virginia French —
read at the dedication of Rugby

Hughes presided at the opening day ceremony, which was attended by friends and dignitaries from Cincinnati, Knoxville, Chattanooga, and New England. Following his address, worship services, and dinner, residents and visitors pursued various entertainments—fishing, playing lawn tennis, enjoying music around the Tabard's new piano, and exchanging war stories.

After the visitors' departure the next morning, Hughes observed:

> By night, Rugby had settled down again to its ordinary life,
> not, however, without a sense of strength gained for the
> work of building up a community which shall know how to
> comport itself in good and bad times, and shall help instead
> of hindering, its sons and daughters in leading a brave,
> simple, and Christian life.

By 1881, The Rugby Stone Quarries Company, Rugby Drug Company, Rugby Printing Works, Partridge Spring Dairy, and the real estate firm of Armstrong & Nairn existed. The Rugby Commissary, the only cooperative effort that was viable for a time, was also in operation.

A Lawn Tennis Club was formed in 1880; the Reading Room was operating by early 1881; and successive years saw the founding of the Philharmonic Society, the Masonic Lodge, Rugby Social Club, Ladies Church Working Society, Rugby Musical and Dramatic Club, and the Cornet Band. Emily Hughes, niece of Thomas Hughes, wrote on October 8, 1882, "The Rugby Cornet Band made its first appearance in public in the evening at the supper. It is almost entirely composed of amateurs and as they have been practising for a very short time, the noise they made was something excrutiating." Tennis, croquet, badminton, and swimming in nearby Clear Fork River remained popular as well as the English custom of taking afternoon tea.

Who were these people who became "Rugbeians?" Initially, most were English or Scotch. About 20 percent were Americans. Some were hard workers, prepared to wait for several years before achieving agricultural success. However, some "second sons" received remittances from home and survived on that instead of setting to work.

above: Early Rugby tennis players.
left: Advertisements from the Rugbeian.

Drawn to Rugby with the promise of an "agreeable temperature in summer" and a "gentle and mild" winter climate, Rugbeians found their first winter the coldest and most severe in 25 years, and their first summer was unusually hot and dry as well. Because of unlucky timing, the settlers' first year in Rugby was extremely difficult.

A sharp frost and snow greeted Christmas morning, 1880. It was the first Christmas in the new colony and for many, it was their first Christmas away from England. The *Rugbeian's* account of that day recounts it favorably: the young men hunted deer and wild turkeys while the young ladies made calls to their neighbors. The only regrets were that the "religious service of praise and thanksgiving could not be had due to the church building not being completed" and that no mistletoe was found. However, the *Rugbeian* stated "it was hoped some friends in the Old Country would forward a few roots of the tree to be planted with due ceremony". Four months later, the newspaper had done its homework and reported that mistletoe was a parasitic plant.

By January 1881, seven inches of snow had already fallen at Rugby — compared to only two inches the entire previous winter. Delivery of supplies was difficult and the *Rugbeian* reported that residents were "all busy planning for the future, comforting each other in whatever afflictions they think they have, and longing for the opening of spring."

The monthly issues of the *Rugbeian* left its readers with a bit of humor and a bright hope for an easier life in this remote mountain village. Advertisements increased in each issue of the paper. The Rugby Stone Quarries Company promised its customers that it was "prepared to supply building stone, flag and hearth stones, window sills, etc. promptly and in any quantity, at very moderate rates." J. F. Mendenhall and Company of Indianapolis, Indiana, offered seeds. Saddles and harnesses could be purchased through Graf & Morsbach in Cincinnati, Ohio, and D. H. Baldwin & Company, also out of Cincinnati, would deliver pianos and organs. There were also advertisements for legal services, surveying, bakeries, watches, and dry goods. Supplies became more easily obtained when Rugby Drug Supply began selling "medicines, perfumery, Whitman's Candies, smoker's requisites, Iced Soda Water, oils and paints, stationery, toys & children's specialities, and groceries."

Published in the February, 1881, *Rugbeian,* the following poem reflected
the community's disillusionment with the weather:

Oh my! Whatever shall we do?
  Zero one day and seven below;
With fingers red and noses blue,
  We 'herd' the stove and watch the snow.

We bless (?) the warm and sunny South,
  Where 'no extremes of cold' are known;
We feel a little down in mouth
  To find our pet delusion flown.

Next day a thaw, and now we toil
  Through mud so deep and slimy—Fudge!
Is this your 'thin and sandy' soil,
  This sticky, binding, greasy sludge?

Rain, drizzle, sleet; plash, drip, drop, swish
  Our wagons sink below the nave,
(Some call it hub); we really wish
  The weather bureau would behave.

But in spite of all the rain and snow,
  On paper we'll our feelings vent;
We'll work, and laugh at earthly woe,
  Nor for the weather care a cent.

—Ovidius Grub

Spring did come, and again the community's difficulties took the form of
poetry in the newspaper:

This is laughing spring time.
  Farewell wintry shakes.
Welcome little blue birds,
  Welcome playful snakes.

On every nose the house-fly
  Perching quite at ease,
Poor bewildered mortals
  Vainly try to seize.

Lean and shadowy porkers
  Grub among the roots.
Dissipated night-owls
  Hiccough out their hoots.

Forth from every tree stump
  Crawls the friendly tick.
To the weary woodsman
  Gives a loving prick.

When too roughly handled
  Little does he mind.
But to show his friendship,
  Leaves his head behind.

Birds and beasts are pairing
  By the water's edge.
Slimy frogs their love songs
  Croak among the sedge.

Black and yellow gad-flies
  Buzz around and sting.
These and other pleasures
  Come in laughing spring.

—Ovidius Grub

Some of Rugby's first settlers.

Throughout that first year, work continued on planning and laying out the town, erecting buildings, and in general making Thomas Hughes' dream become a reality. Due to an ailing wife and other duties, Thomas could not live at Rugby. However, his brother Hastings came to Rugby to contribute whatever he could to its settlement.

The population of Rugby was about 300 in Spring 1881, and a typhoid epidemic broke out in the hot, dry summer that followed. Between August and November, the fever took seven lives including Osmond Dakeyne, one of the *Rugbeian's* editors. The cause of the epidemic was traced to the Hotel Tabard's well in connection with undeveloped public health facilities. Hastings Hughes closed the Tabard in early October with orders to disinfect the entire building "from cellar to dome." The Tabard reopened in late 1881, but the population of Rugby had by that time dropped to under 100.

Just before the typhoid epidemic, Margaret Hughes, the 83-year-old mother of Thomas and Hastings Hughes, arrived in Rugby with her young grand-daughter, Emily. The presence of this elderly matriarch gave strength to the young colony. In the early months of 1882, there was a renewed influx of settlers. With the opening of the Hughes Library on October 5, 1882, which helped revive hopes that the colony would survive and prosper, the population had again risen to 300. By January 1884, the population had increased to about 400.

A cultural society, it was only logical that Rugby would soon see an excellent school open in the community. Affiliated with the University of the South at Sewanee, Tennessee, and under the patronage of the Protestant Episcopal Church of Tennessee, Arnold School for Boys opened January 6, 1885, with six students. It was named for Thomas Arnold, Thomas Hughes' headmaster at Rugby School in England.

"Religious knowledge in harmony with the principles of the Protestant Episcopal Church, English, Latin, Modern Languages, Bookkeeping,

Mathematics, History, Geography, Drawing, Vocal Music and Physical Training" was available for $40 per term, and board (including washing, fire, and lights) was an additional $100.

The December 13, 1884, edition of the *Rugby Gazette and East Tennessee News* ran an advertisement for Arnold School listing the following reasons why boys should be sent to Rugby, Tennessee:

> 1. Acknowledged healthfulness of the climate of the Cumberland Plateau;
> 2. Students will not be grouped in large dormitories but may live with their headmaster, or be placed in families by the Executive Committee where they will have the refinements of a Christian Home;
> 3. Objective of the school is to make its students Christians, Gentlemen, and Scholars;
> 4. Owing to the distance of Rugby from cities, there is no temptation to spend money needlessly and students will be guarded against those evils that surround youth in large towns;
> 5. Highest medical authorities agree that growing boys should spend the earlier part of their lives in pure air and with quiet surroundings: These conditions the Cumberland Plateau affords in marked degree.

Arnold School was only in operation for a few years, and its building is no longer standing.

All was not well in Rugby in 1885. Many "Will Wimbles," a label coined for younger sons with good blood and poor prospects, spent too much time riding, shooting, playing tennis, loafing, and grumbling. The settlers who did work hard were outnumbered. It seemed there were two extremes of English settlers — one group determined to better their lives through hard work, the other predisposed simply to enjoy a good time instead of working for a living as Hughes had intended.

A birthday party for Margaret Hughes, mother of Thomas Hughes.

Other factors that contributed to Rugby's failure to become what Hughes envisioned were mismanagement and poor communication between the London-based Board of Aid and Rugby's on-site managers, less fertile soil than originally thought, heavy forest that needed to be cleared before farming, the severe first winter, the typhoid epidemic the following summer, the promised railroad spur to Rugby that never came about, and unclear titles to land that forced many to wait months before they could begin to use their land. Their deeply-rooted social class distinctions caused some colonists to listen more carefully to their agricultural teacher, a former London butler, than to native Tennessee farmers whose experience could have taught them much more.

Poor planning and lack of business knowledge doomed attempts to found a tomato canning factory, a pottery, and a chicken farm. Sarah Kellogg Walton, the first child born in Rugby, summed up Rugby's failure to fulfill Hughes' vision:

> Perhaps the real reason for the failure of the English Rugby was the fact that the colony started at the top, bent upon enjoying the social and intellectual pleasures before laying a foundation for economic prosperity through industry and self-denial.

The *Rugbeian* said of Hastings Hughes, Thomas' brother, "If the future historian is compelled to write failure at the end of the Rugby Colony, the cause will not be laid at the door of Hastings Hughes." Because of "his rapid riding, driving, walking, talking, writing, from early morning to late at night, and all without apparent annoyance," he gave Rugby all he could. While his brother was "selling" the colony, Hastings was running the colony. Upon his mother's death in 1887, Hastings observed:

> With Mrs. Hughes' death Rugby lost much of its attraction for English settlers. In spite of its beauty and healthfulness it never was a place in which to educate Will Wimbles to hard work, collectively . . . and so, as a settlement, it stagnated. But this much may be said for it now—

An artist's rendering of the utopian garden.

14

that not one of the young Englishmen who came to it, but was better for his Rugby experience, and that nearly all of those who were of any account remained on this side of the water.

Thomas Hughes died in England in 1896. Shortly before his death he wrote: "I can't help feeling and believing that good seed was sown when Rugby was founded. . .and someday the reapers, whoever they may be, will come along with joy bearing heavy sheaves with them."

By 1900 many of the original settlers were gone. The visitors, as many as 1,000 some years, had stopped coming. The English Board of Aid sold out to American interests in 1909. Rugby was never deserted, but "settled down to rest," becoming a quiet, small Tennessee town compared to the flurry of activity and publicity that surrounded its founding.

In the 1920's there were still about a hundred area natives and British residents in the village. They still had dances and bazaars, and enjoyed the Thomas Hughes Library and the Gentlemen's Swimming Hole. The Ladies' Church Working Society and Christ Church were still active.

Will and Sarah Walton, both children of original colonists, refused to consign Rugby to history as another failed utopian experiment. Until their deaths in the 1950's, they helped care for the remaining buildings in their home town. Other residents contributed to Rugby's preservation as well. Oscar Martin came to Rugby by chance in the 1930's and has been in residence every summer since. He and his brother Irving have purchased and protected hundreds of acres of land and some of the original buildings over the years, and both are founding board members of Historic Rugby. Nellie Lender Brooks, wife of Morgan County's first agricultural agent, encouraged the production of local crafts and owned Uffington House, with dreams of making it into a museum. As late as 1963, resident Patricia Wichmann was contributing to the literature written about Rugby by compiling her research in a short history of Rugby entitled *Key to Library*.

Thomas Hughes' dream may never have materialized in the eyes of some, but a young man named Brian Stagg heard whispers of it a century later. He caught the spirit of the dream and made it his own. Though still a teenager,

above: Present-day community center.
right: Colonel and Mrs. Walton and family at Walton Court, circa 1905.

Stagg attempted a "second founding of Rugby" based on the best of its original aims while learning from its early unrealistic idealism.

Just as Hughes had promoted the colony 100 years before, Brian began to talk to local groups and correspond with senators and government officials. Through his intense efforts, Rugby began to awaken. He began to compile a history of the community and its people, instilling in them the dream to rebuild, to restore, and to share the rich heritage and hope upon which Rugby was founded. Brian's life was short, and he worked with an unceasing determination to make Rugby known to those who would care for and preserve it. It seems fitting that Brian, himself a second son, took the responsibility to begin the revival of Rugby, created partly for the benefit of second sons of a less fortunate era.

Time passed. Rugby remained. The dream survived. Present day Rugbeians still cherish the dream. In his opening day address, Thomas Hughes asked that Rugby be treated lovingly and reverently. That love and reverence still permeate the air, for the dream is again becoming a reality.

Who lives in Rugby today? About 65 people call the Victorian village home. Non-profit Historic Rugby is the main employer in the immediate area. The surrounding area provides employment mainly in the timber, mining, oil and gas industries. Some citizens are raising young families; others are building homes for retirement. All seem to have a sense of pride in their community.

Most Rugbeians have an appreciation for what Rugby could become. Plans are to preserve the small rural town atmosphere with hopes to rebuild, but not exceed, its early population. Other goals are to continue the restoration of the village, to protect its historic heritage, and to develop and expand services to meet the demands of growth.

As Rugby enters the 21st century, its residents envision a permanently-preserved historic site. With parking away from the historic area and the main highway rerouted, visitors and residents alike would be free to walk the length of the village and enjoy the homes and shops of its first century. Private development of historically compatible shops and services would be encouraged when numbers of visitors will support them. Homesites where historically compatible houses can be built will be available in the future. Rugby is still "open to all who like our ways."

Rugby's magic is contagious, and, once caught, is not easily dispelled. It was stated best by Brian Stagg in *The Distant Eden*:

> The most remarkable aspect of Rugby is a certain indwelling of spirit. Even the visitor, not generally prone to poetic sentiment, should feel Rugby's spell. If he will visit the Library on a breezy summer afternoon and wait for twilight's approach, he might sense, lingering in the air, the presence of a melancholy but benevolent spirit that refuses to let go of the glory that was Rugby.

RUGBY SCHOOLHOUSE

The first school building was constructed in 1880. Three stories tall, it had a double staircase, wainscot and plaster interior, Gothic windows and a large stained glass window on the third floor. Several denominations used the second floor for worship services, and the third floor was used by the Masons and Oddfellows.

Destroyed by fire in 1906, it was rebuilt on the same site the following year. The second building is not as elaborate. It is only two stories with steep, narrow stairs. School was held here until 1951.

Historic Rugby has completed restoration of the schoolhouse for use as a visitor center and offices. From here visitors may begin a tour of Rugby and see a most interesting exhibit that traces the history of Rugby from its inception to its restoration.

THOMAS HUGHES FREE PUBLIC LIBRARY

"When his work is done, he will find himself in a cultivated society, within easy reach of all the real essentials of civilisation, beginning with a good library," said Thomas Hughes of Rugby's colonists.

Opened to the public on October 5, 1882, the library met an essential need of the cultured Rugbeians. Visitors browsing through the library today are delighted to see the rare and extensive collection of books—over 7,000 volumes—some of which are first editions. The oldest volume was printed in 1687 and no books published later than 1899 are on its shelves. It is one of the best representative collections of Victorian literature in America.

20

The colonists had a wide selection of subjects. Books of interest to women and children were available as well as agricultural reports and advice for many men's new farming ventures. Newspapers and magazines were also available for the pleasure and entertainment of Rugbeians and their guests.

The library has never had electricity and never been heated except for short periods. Its natural levels of humidity and heat and cold, combined with its unique ventilation system, seem to have preserved the books. Few are faded, and most are in good condition.

Approaching the library today, one can almost see an "out to lunch" sign swinging from the doorknob. Upon entering, it appears that everyone has indeed stepped out for just a few minutes and will return momentarily. Listening, one can almost hear the chairs being pulled up to the tables, pages being softly turned, and low voices murmuring about the adventures found beyond this window of the world.

CHRIST CHURCH EPISCOPAL

Christ Church was formally organized by the Right Reverend Charles Todd Quintard, Bishop of Tennessee of the Protestant Episcopal Church, on the same day Rugby was officially opened—October 5, 1880. Seven years later, October 16, 1887, the beautiful little church building was completed and opened for service. Today it is still serving as a place of worship for Rugbeians and visitors. Within its serene and peaceful walls, time seems to stop. The bustle and hurry of the 20th century seem totally removed as the visitor lingers in this holy place.

Symbolism and traditionalism abound in Christ Church. An apse, a three-sided extension, surrounds the altar as is traditional in the Carpenter's Gothic architectural style. The chancel and nave are divided by a 'rood beam,' a large beam over the steps. "Rood" is a Middle English word for "cross," and Christ Church, in keeping with tradition, has a cross bearing a cristogram mounted on this beam.

The native yellow pine paneling has darkened with age and makes the stained glass window even more dominant as time passes. This window was made in Germany and was donated to the church in 1889 by Bishop Quintard. The left panel of the window is dedicated to Margaret Hughes, mother of Thomas Hughes, and the right panel is dedicated to Mary Blacklock, mother of Reverend Joseph Blacklock, first rector of the church. The two Greek letters in the window, Alpha and Omega, signify God, the beginning and the end, and the elements of bread and wine in Communion are represented by the shock of wheat and grapes.

The original and unrestored "fleurs de lis" on either side of the altar are actually symbols of the Holy Trinity. The brass cross, candlesticks, and vases brought by the colonists from England were in use continuously until 1979, and have been replaced by similar items from a village church near Hughes' birthplace in England.

Cornelius Onderdonk, the architect who designed the church, made the Baptismal Font which is still in use as well as all the hand carved black walnut altar furniture. Also in service still are the alms basins, one of which was carved in 1884 by Thomas Hughes' childhood friend Henry Fry. Incised on the back of the basin is the quotation, "For the love of Tom Brown," a reference to *Tom Brown's School Days*. Fry also carved Queen Victoria's throne, and restored some carvings in the White House and at Mount Vernon.

The hanging lamps, electrified in the 1950's, were also brought from England by early colonist William Henry Gilliat. Of his family left in England, one was a member of Parliament. However, the Gilliat family formed strong bonds for their new home and today Mr. Gilliat's great grandson is residing in Rugby and has served as Historic Rugby's Properties Director for a decade.

Made in London in 1849, the solid rosewood harmonium reed organ is the oldest of its type still in use in the United States. In recent years it has been electrified.

Many people through the years have lovingly given their time and talent to preserve this quiet retreat from modern day pressures. Today's worshipers are still summoned by the old English ship's bell.

KINGSTONE LISLE

Kingstone Lisle, a small village near Uffington, England, where he grew up, was the name Thomas Hughes chose for his new home in Rugby. Every fall Hughes would visit Rugby and stay for one or two months. After staying at Pioneer Cottage, the Tabard Hotel, or his mother's Uffington House, his own home was completed in time for his annual visit in 1885. Hughes returned to Kingstone Lisle again in 1886 and 1887. After his mother's death in 1887, he never returned to Rugby.

Visitors touring Kingstone Lisle will note trunks which reflect Hughes' constant traveling during each visit. On display in the parlor is a square grand Weber piano built in 1866 which was one of the seven original pianos in the colony, a stereoscope and slides from the 1880's, and a chess set carved in Germany and brought to Rugby by one of the colonists.

English primroses, Michaelmas Daisies, and Lilies of the Valley still bloom in the yard.

The dining room contains pieces original to Rugby. The huge chestnut china closet is from Twin Oaks, the cherry tables and circular dining table are from Newbury House, and the sideboard is from Uffington House.

Upon entering the kitchen, it is impossible not to recall memories or tales of old wood stoves. The Kalamazoo Queen cook stove, which once fed lodgers at Newbury House, boasts a warming oven, a side mounted hot-water heater, and a temperature gauge.

The bedroom also has some original furnishings. The carved walnut bed is from Twin Oaks; both the nightstand and the chest of drawers are from the Tabard; and the writing table is from Uffington. The French marble-top dresser may be original to Kingstone Lisle, as no one can remember its not being in the house. The set of china on the nightstand, the bedspread, and the quilt are all from the Victorian period.

PERCY COTTAGE

Sir Henry Kimber, a close friend of Thomas Hughes, was a wealthy barrister and a chief financial backer of the colony. He had Percy Cottage built in 1884 and named it for his son, Percy.

Present day Percy Cottage is an historic reconstruction that was completed in 1977. The downstairs rooms are filled with gifts and books—many on Rugby and the Victorian era -- and all are available for purchase.

HARROW ROAD CAFE

The October 1881 *Rugbeian* reported:

> A cafe has been started in Harrow Road by a couple of enterprising young Englishmen and meals can be obtained there at any time between the hours of 8 A.M. and 10 P.M. They have a long and varied list of comestibles, and, as far as we can judge. . .are likely to drive a "roaring trade."

Today, Historic Rugby operates the Harrow Road Cafe, the third to stand on the site. Built in 1985 to conform with Rugby's historic architecture, the cafe's ceiling fans and working fireplaces lend a welcome touch whatever the weather. Rugby's residents and visitors can enjoy traditional Cumberland Plateau cooking and British Isles specialties. The cafe seats 80 and is open daily, year-round, except Thanksgiving, Christmas, and New Year's Day.

RUGBY PRINTING WORKS

Shortly after the opening of Rugby in 1880, the Rugby Printing Works published the first issue of the *Rugbeian* newspaper in January, 1881. The paper was continuously published, usually weekly, for the next seven years under several changes of name and ownership. The type had to be set by hand. The "job" press was operated by a foot treadle or, for long runs, by a steam engine.

Today's Rugby Printing Works, a delightfully detailed Victorian building, stands just across the road from the first one. It was built in the 1880's in nearby Deer Lodge and moved to Rugby in 1979 because of historical connections and its similarity to the original Rugby shop. Currently open primarily during special events, the restored building will eventually be open daily during tour season as a working Victorian-era printing office.

RUGBY COMMISSARY

Only a little more than ten months after the Commissary opened, the *Rugbeian* reported in late August, 1882:

> Crowded out of the old log cabin by the great pressure of business, the new commissary building was erected . . . to meet the pressing wants of the colony. The new store is situated on Central Avenue and presents an excellent appearance . . .. The whole cost of the building must have been nearly $3,000.

Over the store was "The Hall" which was available for meetings, dinners, and entertainment.

Today's reconstructed Commissary has been faithfully reproduced by Historic Rugby even down to the rocking chairs on the front veranda. The first floor has a variety of craft items made by area residents. These crafts, rocking chairs, wooden items, quilts, baskets, and dolls to name a few, are all available for purchase. Also for sale are British Isle favorites such as Scotch Shortbread, Dundee's Marmalade, lemon curd, English toffee, Cadbury Cocoa, and old-time Watkins products.

The large upstairs room serves as a classroom for the various crafts taught throughout the year. Historic Rugby provides information on opportunities to learn spinning, weaving, candlemaking, basketry, needlework, quilting, and other crafts which are showcased in the Annual Rugby Spring Music and Crafts Festival.

PIONEER COTTAGE

The first frame structure in town, this original building dates from 1880. It was here that many young Englishmen spent their first weeks in Rugby. Thomas Hughes' first night at Rugby was spent here. In his book *Rugby, Tennessee* Hughes described his life at pioneer cottage with its mischievous young men. It is no wonder it was often referred to as "The Asylum" until it was renamed Pioneer Cottage to capture the spirit of the Rugby venture.

Over the years it has served as a makeshift drug store and as the headquarters for the Musical and Dramatic Club. During the typhoid epidemic, and again after the fire that destroyed the Tabard, it became an important boarding house.

Restored by Historic Rugby, Pioneer Cottage is again available for overnight lodging. With its parlor, three bedrooms, fully equipped kitchen and modern baths, Pioneer Cottage's 20th-century guests enjoy comforts only dreamed about 100 years ago.

NEWBURY HOUSE

Even before the English Board of Aid to Land Ownership took over Rugby, Newbury House (then called Brown House) was open for business. It remained a favorite place for dining and lodging even after the Tabard was opened in 1881. In 1884 the Tabard burned leaving Newbury once again the only sizable lodging facility in Rugby.

Emily Hughes saw Miss Dyer, a servant from England, leave Uffington House to take over management of Newbury House in 1883. She wrote to Willy Hughes in April, 1884, "the Newbury House . . . is quite full now and they have 15 or 20 people at most times. . ." The Kellogg family, whose daughter was the first child born in Rugby, took in guests as late as the 1920's.

Reopened in May 1985, after extensive restoration by Historic Rugby, the Victorian charm and hospitality of early Rugby is again available for overnight guests to enjoy.

TWIN OAKS

Beriah Riddell, a skilled builder by trade, completed the main part of his home in 1882. Its high ceilings allowed for interior transoms over all the doors on the first floor permitting cross ventilation. Instead of pine paneling like other Rugby homes, Twin Oaks' rooms were plastered. The upstairs study had a parquet floor.

This elegant house was often referred to as the "Mansion House." In the evenings 27 kerosene lamps and chandeliers were kept burning.

The *Rugbeian* gave these accounts of Twin Oaks:

> April 8, 1882—"approaching completion"
>
> May 13, 1882—"Mr. Riddell has moved into his new and pretty villa."
>
> December 23, 1882—"Mr. and Mrs. Riddell gave an elegant dinner in celebration of Mr. Riddell's 35th birthday."

In 1883 the Riddells closed their home due to Mr. Riddell's illness. He sought care in Chattanooga and returned six months later.

A gifted builder, Mr. Riddell seems to have worked exclusively on finishing touches for his own home for two years. Records indicate Mr. Riddell did not work on another building until May, 1884.

Twin Oaks, one of the soundest houses still standing in Rugby, underwent extensive restoration in the late 1960's.

UFFINGTON HOUSE

The home of Madam Hughes and her granddaughter Emily from 1881-1887, Uffington House was bought by Hastings Hughes, Emily's father and Thomas' brother. It was originally only a small cottage which today serves as the entrance hall.

Before the Hughes ladies moved in, two rooms were added. Throughout the following year, more additions and alterations were made to accommodate the cook, maid, butler, and gardener who came from England with Mrs. Hughes.

Dissipations At Uffington House, a collection of letters written by Emily Hughes from her upstairs bedroom, tells of her love for the farmyard animals she raised, of planting flowers in the yard, and of her trial and error way of learning photography. The picture emerges of a young girl somewhat lonely for her English friends and old way of life, yet excited about the new colony.

After Margaret Hughes' death in 1887, the house and outbuildings were offered for sale at a price of $4,000. The house included a drawing room, dining room, kitchen, pantry (with cellar below), and hall on the first floor with a stove or fireplace in each room. Upstairs were six bedrooms with stoves in three. A veranda ran along the front and one side of the house.

The outbuildings included a two-room house with loft, a stable, carriage house, and a chicken house.

If the buyer had doubts about the location, the sale notice had this to say of Rugby:

> Town of Rugby in which the property is situated is unexcelled as a health resort and surrounded by scenery which is unsurpassed. Capital hunting and fishing, riding, driving, and other out-door amusements....
> The town is 7 miles from the depot and contains two churches, stores, first class public library, large hotel, livery stable, lawn tennis grounds, etc.

Today, guests walk under its rustic arbor to the front door where the original doorknocker with its Latin inscription "Flourish Rugby" continues to alert Uffington's occupants of their arrival.

ADENA COTTAGE

Built about 1884, Adena still stands today. It was given its name by its first occupant, Mrs. Wellman, the former Sarah Worthington Pomeroy. She was the granddaughter of Governor Worthington of Ohio and named Adena for the family home in Ohio.

Adena was graced with many beautiful pieces of art and antiques acquired by the Wellmans in their travels associated with Mr. Wellman's occupation as a tea merchant.

The Wellman family moved to Rugby with the expectation that Mr. Wellman's health would improve in the pure mountain air. This charming family had a son and two daughters. The girls, Edith and Eleanor, and their mother are buried in Rugby's Laurel Dale Cemetery.

The Helen Lourie family lived at Adena from the 1920's through the 1970's. Today Adena is again home to a lovely family. Children once again laugh and dream and play within the walls of stately Adena.

left: Adena at the turn of the century.

below: Adena today.

WREN'S NEST

Originally planned to be an elaborate "hennery,"the Wren's Nest was built around 1887 on the Wellman property in back of Adena. Mr. Wellman was the secretary of the Rugby Poultry Company which was chartered in 1886.

Built at the edge of a ravine, the Wren's Nest offers its occupants a view that gives a sense of being suspended in mid-air as dozens of flowering trees bloom below.

A cozy dwelling with a living room, dining room, kitchen, and a narrow stairway with a circular turn leading to two bedrooms, the Wren's Nest is currently being restored by its new owner.

INGLESIDE

Oriental art objects filled Ingleside in the 1880's. Russell Sturgis, first U.
S. Counsel to Canton, China, and his wife traveled extensively during his career
collecting art before retiring to Rugby.

Ingleside was built in 1884 and consists of seven rooms. A bay window is
at each end of the house and a winding stairway leads to three upstairs
chambers.

The house has also been called the Hemlocks for the trees "which grace
its portals."

THE LINDENS

The Lindens was the home of Nathan Tucker, first manager of the Rugby Commissary. It was built in 1880 and named for the huge European linden trees that shade it.

An avid flower lover, Mrs. Tucker grew flowers in the glass enclosed sun porch at the front of the home. Her beautiful arrangements could be seen year round in Christ Church.

The carriage house behind the Lindens is one of the most architecturally interesting outbuildings in Rugby.

Will and Esther Walton lived here from the early 1900's until their deaths in the 1950's. According to Oscar Martin, they were truly the "keepers of Rugby."

The carriage house behind the Lindens.

WALTON COURT

A delightful family, the Waltons knew how to entertain and enjoyed raising their large family in a country atmosphere with horses, dogs, donkeys, and a large dairy herd. This large family was the first in Rugby to have a telephone. Robert Walton named his Rural Gothic style home for his ancestral home in Ireland.

Mr. Walton lived here from 1881, the year Walton Court was built, until his death in 1907. A member of the Board of Hughes Public Library, a Lay Reader for Christ Church, and a member of the Masonic Lodge, Mr. Walton contributed much to Rugby as the town's business manager and head surveyor. He laid out the lots and roads. Upon his death, his son Will took over the care and management of what was left of Rugby.

ROSLYN

Named after Roslyn Castle in Scotland, this home was built in 1886 by John Boyle, the first (and very unpopular) business manager of the colony. Its Georgian style is complemented by Victorian decorative elements.

All interior pine-paneled walls, floors, and ceilings are original. The date of the addition to the rear is not known. A large hall, extending the depth of the house, was often used for dancing. The Tysons, Roslyn's first occupants, enjoyed entertaining. Jesse Tyson would drive a four horse talley-ho and speed down High Street to deliver guests for parties at Roslyn.

Stories have been told of hearing horses on the gravel driveway in this century, 100 years later. Some residents report seeing a black talley-ho carriage race up the driveway, make a circle in front of the house and dash off through the dense woods on the exact path High Street had run in Tyson's day. Other rumors say Jesse's sister, Sophie, walks the hall, crying. Research has not provided any clues as to why Sophie's crying continues in this century.

LAUREL DALE CEMETERY

Laurel Dale was donated to the colony by the Board of Aid and consecrated by Bishop Quintard. It is still in use and is free to community residents. As in the 19th century, it is beautifully maintained by the Laurel Dale Cemetery Association.

The first person to be buried in Laurel Dale Cemetery was a little child. In 1885, little Grace, only four days past her first birthday, was laid to rest. Tombstones tell of the tragic loss of other lives: seven victims of the typhoid epidemic; 36-year-old Adam Burroughs who drowned in the Clear Fork River in 1886; babies from four days old to 17 months old; a seven year old boy and his 11 month old sister.

Also found here are many who had long full lives such as Margaret Hughes, 90 years old. Many war veterans are also here. The wars they fought were the Civil War (both Union and Confederate soldiers), World Wars I and II and the Spanish-American War.

above: Oak Lodge, originally called the White House, served as an overflow guest house.
below: Ruralia, built by Daniel Elleby circa 1884.

BOARD OF AID TO LAND OWNERSHIP

The Board of Aid was the center of all the colony's business activity. Colonists came here to buy land, borrow money, look for work, send a telegram, or rent a house.

Upon completion in 1880, the *Rugbeian* stated the Board of Aid looked like a cross between a rural chapel and a railway station. Restored by Historic Rugby in 1976, it served as its headquarters and archives until it was destroyed by arson the following year. All that remains of the Board of Aid today is the stone foundation and dreams of eventual rebuilding.

TABARD INN

Named for the inn in Chaucer's Canterbury Tales, the Tabard boasted a balustrade from the original Tabard. Built in the early 1880's, it served as lodging for the many people visiting Rugby and as a temporary home for residents awaiting completion of their houses.

Rugby was becoming a popular vacation resort. An advertisement in the June 1883 *Rugbeian* listed the following attractions for visitors:

> — Cool, bracing, healthful mountain air
> — Woods abounding in game -deer, turkey, pheasants, quail, squirrel
> — Fishing and bathing in the clear river near the hotel
> — Amusements of all kinds -lawn tennis, croquet, ball games, swings, etc.
> — The elegant Hughes Public Library -free
> — Fresh fruits and vegetables in abundance from the English gardens adjoining hotel grounds
> — Charming walks and views along the river
> — The hotel is beautifully located in its own enclosure of five acres of grassy lawn, flower beds, play grounds, pet deer park and native forest trees, having wide double veranda on three sides
> — Pleasant, light, airy rooms, completely furnished and excellent, wholesome, home-like board at very reasonable prices
> — Round trip tickets from Cincinnati or Chattanooga over the Cincinnati Southern Railway at low rates.

When the Tabard opened in 1880, rates were $2/day, $10/week, and $30/month.

At the peak of its popularity, the Tabard Inn burned to the ground on October 16, 1884. A larger, more elaborate Tabard was built and opened June 7, 1887. Musical concerts were enjoyed every afternoon and evening and its advertisements flaunted a "refined society" where patrons of the old Tabard "will find the New Tabard a gem in its sphere, where all the luxeries of the city are combined with a quiet home in this favored mountain retreat."

The second Tabard also succumbed to fire. Historic Rugby plans to rebuild the first Tabard Inn. Upon its completion, the building that has been both the pride and sorrow of Rugby, and the focal point of its disasters, will once again take prominence as one of the town's main attractions.

left: A survey party on the porch of the original Board of Aid Building.

below: Artist's rendering of the first Tabard Inn.

WHEN YOU VISIT

What is in store for the 20th century visitor to Rugby? Informative tours are conducted by congenial and knowledgeable guides. Beginning at the Schoolhouse Visitor Centre, which contains a wealth of information and history about Rugby dating back to its founding, the visitor to Rugby can step back into the dignity of the Victorian era by touring the Thomas Hughes Library, Christ Church, and Kingstone Lisle, the home built for Thomas Hughes.

Century-old trails abound in this wooded area. Hike down to the Gentlemen's Swimming Hole in the Clear Fork River gorge. Walk down the packed gravel and dirt roads. Experience the serenity of the countryside as cows graze idly in the quiet air.

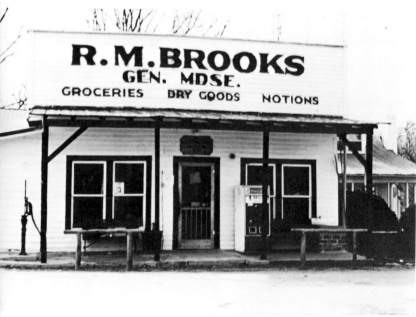

An annual Rugby Spring Music and Crafts Festival occurs in mid-May. Craftsworkers sell and demonstrate blacksmithing, basketry, needlework, candlemaking, weaving, dollmaking, quilting, spinning, and other types of traditional and Victorian handicrafts. British Isles and Appalachian music, dancing, and plenty of good food make this a popular time.

For two decades, the Historic Rugby Pilgrimage of Homes has been held during the first weekend in August. This is the only time of the year visitors can tour some of the private homes in Rugby. In addition to the tour of homes, there are concerts, slide programs, and other cultural events.

Rugby celebrates Christmas the old-fashioned way. Lantern tours, festive caroling, inspiring worship, and plenty of good food make Christmas at Rugby an event to look forward to year after year. Christmas at Rugby is open only to members of Historic Rugby, Inc., and only by reservation.

Shopping in the Commissary is an enjoyable experience. A variety of crafts, books, and gifts is for sale and shopkeepers are eager to answer questions and help the shopper make selections. Area residents supply the Commissary with crafts and Historic Rugby offers classes throughout the year which teach traditional crafts of the Plateau.

RUGBY COMMISSARY

— FURNISHES FOR THE —

People of Rugby

AND VICINITY A LARGE ASSORTMENT OF

MERCHANDISE

OF NEARLY EVERY DESCRIPTION AT

LOWEST MARKET PRICES.

—— A Full Supply of ——

Dry and Fancy Goods,

LADIES', GENTS', AND CHILDREN'S

Boots and Shoes of all grades.

A FINE ASSORTMENT OF

CLOTHING AND HATS FOR ALL AGES,

Crockery and Glassware, Hardware and Farming Implements, Woodware, Tinware, &c.

WHICH TOGETHER WITH A FULL LINE OF

GROCERIES

Always on Hand,

Makes the largest and best assortment to be found on the Cumberland Mountain.

N. H. TUCKER, MANAGER.

The Rugby Commissary provided settlers with many necessities.

Historic Rugby conducts daily guided walking tours from March 1 -December 15, with tours sometimes available other times by appointment. Lodging in historic buildings is available year-round, as is food service at the Harrow Road Cafe.

Membership support is vital to Historic Rugby's continuing efforts to restore, preserve, and protect the unique Victorian village. Benefits include free admission to Spring Festival and Annual Pilgrimage of Homes and the opportunity to share Christmas at Rugby. For information on membership, lodging, events, and group tours, contact Historic Rugby, Inc., P.O. Box 8, Rugby, TN 37733, (615) 628-2441.

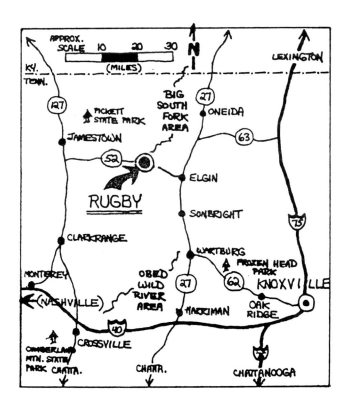

INDEX

Works Consulted:

Dissipations at Uffington House by Emily Hughes
Distant Eden by Brian Stagg
Key to Library by Patricia Wichmann
Letter of John Boyle, Esq., to the Boston Board of Aid to Land Ownership, 1878
Master Plan for the Development, Management, and Protection of the Rugby Colony Historic Area
Plateau Gazette, 1884-87
Plateau Gazette and East Tennessee News, 1883
The Rugbeian, 1881
The Rugby & District Reporter, 1882
Rugby News, 1890
Rugby, Tennessee by Thomas Hughes
Rugby, Tennessee: Monument to Failure or Living Legacy? by Betty Duggan
Thomas Hughes by George Worth
Thomas Hughes Public Library by Douglas Kirke Gordon
Tom Brown's School Days by Thomas Hughes
Visions of Utopia by John Egerton